MONTANA

from the Big Sky

◆

**A Collection of Aerial Photography
by Larry Mayer of the Billings Gazette
with Foreword by Tom Brokaw**

◆

Photos by Larry Mayer

© 1990, *The Billings Gazette*, A division of Lee Enterprises, Inc.

Published by *The Billings Gazette*
Wayne Schile, Publisher
Richard J. Wesnick, Editor

Library of Congress Catalog Card Number 90-083764
ISBN 0-9627618-1-8

For extra copies of the book contact:
The Billings Gazette, P.O. Box 36300, Billings, MT 59107-6300,
In Montana 1-800-332-7089, In Wyoming, Washington, Oregon, Idaho,
North Dakota, and South Dakota, 1-800-325-4298, Elsewhere (406) 657-1200
Book Design by Len Eckel, Len Visual Design
Cover Design by Ben D. Leonard
Printed by Fenske Printing, Inc., Billings, Montana

Printed in the U.S.A.

Aerial Photo of Larry Mayer by Jim Woodcock of The Billings Gazette

Larry Mayer, award-winning chief photographer for The Billings Gazette, is as much at home in the cockpit of his Cessna 180 as he is behind a camera.

"Montana From The Big Sky" is the offspring of his passionate love affair with flying and photography. Sweeping high over Montana, from one far-flung corner to the other, he has captured the essence of this great land on film.

Mayer joined The Gazette staff in 1977. His work has appeared in The New York Times, Geo, Time, Newsweek, U.S. News and World Report, American West, Associated Press, United Press International, National Wildlife, National Geographic World and National Geographic's book on Yellowstone National Park.

Additionally, he contributed to other recent books including "Montana On My Mind," which was published by The Billings Gazette and Falcon Press, and to "Yellowstone On Fire!," "The Big Drive" and "Wagons Across Wyoming" which were published by The Billings Gazette.

Most of the aerial photographs in this book were taken from Mayer's Cessna 180, although some were taken from hot air balloons.

The introduction and captions for this book were written by Roger Clawson, a free-lance writer, syndicated columnist and former Gazette reporter.

Foreword
By
Tom Brokaw

Photo by Rick Graetz

Tom and Meredith Brokaw atop the Chinese Wall.

With all due respect to my friends who worked so hard to publish this magnificent book about Montana, no picture, however artfully framed or printed, no words, however carefully chosen, can adequately capture the magnificence of this rare combination of water and land, mountain and prairie, urban and rural community, man and beast. So why am I attempting this exercise?

A couple of reasons, really. First, I find almost anything about Montana irresistible, including writing about it. Also, in some small way, I hope to share with you that which cannot be conveyed through pictures and their captions.

Take the spirit of Montana. It is at once abstract and yet tangible, an unseen force that provides an extra dimension to the awesome physical properties of the state. It is not a place for the meek. There's nothing tentative about Montana. Consequently it requires boldness and self confidence to meet on even terms its awesome physical properties and meteorological challenges.

While it seems incomprehensible now, it wasn't until I was in my mid 30s that I made my first extensive foray onto the land beneath the Big Sky. A week-long backpacking trip in the Scapegoat Wilderness proved to be an infectious experience. Montana entered my bloodstream. I find the only effective cures are regular visitations to almost any place within its borders. Any place.

A mountain peak in the Absaroka range with a ferocious storm racing up a basin from the south, bringing rain, hail and then a symphony of sunlight, thunderheads and sky. A herd of elk crossing the Sun River in the Bob Marshall Wilderness in ocher, predawn light. A 20-inch rainbow exploding from the turbulent waters of the Madison River just north of Slide Lake. A grizzly bear foraging through huckleberry bushes on the southern flank of Glacier National Park. A rancher and his hired hand of 20 years shyly discussing their brotherhood of work and shared values on a modest spread south of the Stillwater River. A cowboy band in the Road Kill Cafe outside of McLeod. Side by side main street merchants in Bozeman discussing that day's "Doonesbury" strip and their summer reading list. A Blackfeet Indian walking along a lonely road at dusk, a pilgrim from Montana's past, a traveler to an uncertain destination.

Occasionally I feel a little foolish about my attachment to Montana. It seems a childish thing. When I return from a visit to Montana I have to restrain myself when colleagues and friends make a casual inquiry. "How was it? Did you have a good time?" It was wonderful, I'll respond. Yes, I had a very good time. How can I tell them? How can they understand unless they've been there? I want to sit them down and say, "Listen to me! This is important! You're my friend. I want you to know: Montana IS the last best place. They're not making this kind of land any more."

That would be inappropriate, of course. First, Montanans know what they have and if others don't, tough. Montanans, unlike their neighbors in that big cowboy state on the southern border of the United States, aren't much given to unseemly boasting. Second, even if you've never been there, you can visit Montana through the eyes of so many gifted writers who have shared their vision of its glories: Guthrie, McGuane, Welch, Ford, McFadden, Doig, Maclean, Chatham.

It seems to me that is an overlooked measure of the state's attractions. Writers, after all, can live anywhere. They're also a finicky group. I mean, anyone who'd spend most of a morning on the construction of a paragraph can fairly be called finicky, right? And yet can you name another state with so few people and so many gifted writers? Moreover, so far as I can tell, Montana has a leveling effect on writers. The physical properties of the state and the no nonsense style of its citizens humbles writers in a way. That is not an insignificant achievement.

As for me, I can be transported to Montana just by opening a map and letting my mind wander from one border to another. From Plentywood in the northeast to Hungry Horse in the northwest. From Wisdom on the Big Hole River to Sweet Grass County on the Boulder River. Whitefish, Big Timber, Opportunity, Wolf Point, Roundup, Cut Bank, Chinook. In some cases they may be much more than a main street, a hardware store, a bar, a gas station and a church, but those are towns you're not likely to forget.

Who can resist a state with a mountain range called the Crazies? A state that is the source of the mighty Missouri River? The home of Glacier National Park, arguably one of the most scenic wilderness areas anywhere in the world. Amber waves of grain? Check out northeast Montana in mid-summer. This is America singing. Custer died here. Gary Cooper was born here. Remington and Russell and Bodmer gave us Montana in bronze and oil and water color. It's the hunting ground of the Crow, the Assiniboine, Gros Ventre, Blackfeet.

My only regret is that I didn't get to Montana earlier, maybe two hundred years earlier. Since I didn't, I am comforted in knowing there are places in the state where I can clear a rise, emerge from a forest, cross a river and for just a moment believe I am there two hundred years ago. As you'll see in these pages, Montana is never out of season nor out of place.

Tom Brokaw

NBC News Anchorman

Introduction

By

Roger Clawson

Montana's majesty sprawls over nearly 150,000 square miles. Her sons, daughters and lovers know her by touch and feel, by the haughty sweep of her horizon and her reflection in the sky. To each she offers a different facet: one to the miner who scratches her bones, another to the farmer who turns the loam once trod by the woolly mammoth, yet another to the young lovers walking through lupine, Indian paintbrush and shooting stars in an alpine meadow.

This book offers a face of the land known best by the eagle, hawk and those men and women who love her best as the firmament beneath an ocean of air. Secret wonders fill a pilot's heart. No land-bound slave has seen the chinook chase the snows from the breast of the mountains, spiraled downward to witness a mare's tail of summer rain brush the earth or felt the rough texture of the prairie while soaring, buffeted by thermals, across the Golden Triangle.

Turning their backs on heaven to gaze into her face, the pilot and eagle find Montana a land of kaleidoscopic wonder, of mountain rivers dashing themselves to froth and rainbows in a race to the plains, of the deep relief of canyons, coulees and valleys, of vistas to paralyze the lungs and impose upon the heart a rhythm erratic as Montana's seasons.

From the air, she is a land defined neither by fences nor political boundaries. From the air, space is a collage of watersheds, each defined by its own divide and fitted with precision into the cluster of its neighbors. From the air, time is evening puddled in the draws while dusk chases sun's last light into the highlands.

This book is your opportunity to share the cockpit with Larry Mayer, veteran Billings Gazette photographer and a native with Montana in his heart and adventure in his soul. Few have known the great lady more intimately.

Mayer has flown over forest fire and flood, tracked the wheat harvest north into Saskatchewan and flirted with cloud-busting peaks.

While auto exhaust and a view of Main Street may constitute the pedestrian's memory of a city, Mayer sees cities, ranches, even forests and mountain ranges in the context of their settings.

Join Mayer in this grand view. What you see through this flier's eyes will never appear the same again.

(Next page) The moon hurries to bury itself in the Western horizon as the rising sun highlights limestone cliffs of Bighorn Lake National Recreation Area.

(Above) An Amtrak passenger train glides out of the mountains of Glacier National Park and rolls past East Glacier on its way toward the prairies of Eastern Montana.

(Left) The Bridger Mountains loom over valleys and hollows. Named for the mountain man Jim Bridger who guided white gold seekers into Montana.

(Next page) Fall colors gild the Tongue River as it flows through Cheyenne country toward Montana's cow capital, Miles City.

Trapped between the Absaroka Mountains and a cloud bank, the setting sun spills molten gold along the horizon.

Snow swirling from Granite Peak is set ablaze by a winter sun. Flagship of the Beartooth Mountains, Granite Peak rises 12,799 feet above sea level, the highest point in the state.

Sunrise's alchemy turns Medicine Lake to silver. Protected by the U.S. Fish and Wildlife Service, a wealth of shorebirds nest along these scalloped shores south of Plentywood.

Day's last light washes the limestone cliffs of the Pryor Mountains. Named for Sgt. Pryor of the Lewis and Clark Expedition, these unique mountains are the home of a herd of wild horses and, according to Crow Indian legend, dwelling place of the supernatural Little People.

Cottonwoods cluster in the bends of the Powder River. Meandering through Eastern Montana cattle country that overlies the great coal deposits of Montana and Wyoming, the Powder is said to be "a mile wide and an inch deep, too thick to drink and too thin to plow."

Suburbia sprawls where sagebrush recently flourished. Coyotes and antelope shared this land before developers transformed it into Billings Heights.

Granite ridges of the Crazy Mountains stand naked in the gale as wind makes plumes of high country snow. It was in these sacred mountains that Plenty Coup, Crow Indian chief of chiefs, had a vision foretelling the coming of European civilization.

Winter wind harries the snow that fell as powder on the granite shoulders of the Beartooth Mountains. While ridges are swept clean, mountain meadows and pockets collect the snow that will melt in spring to feed streams coursing toward the lowlands.

(Next page) The Rocky Mountain Front rises sharply from the Great Plains in Blackfeet Country west of Choteau. Nowhere is the transition from prairie to the Continental Divide more precipitous. The Front compresses a succession of ecological zones into a single locality and bares to the world the geologic history of eons past.

Stacks of lumber rest in a mill yard
near Livingston. Timber that spent 100 years
growing may pass another century
as the shell of a home.

Shadows cast by winter's oblique
sunlight streak wheat fields fringed with
shelter belts near Laurel. On arid prairies,
strip farming uses two year's precipitation to
raise one year's crop.

(Right) Dying trees create a gold-on-green mosaic near Libby. Drought and age produce the stress that allows insects and disease to flourish. The condition is but a phase in the ancient cycle of the forest's life, one that invites wildfire to clear the land for another generation of trees.

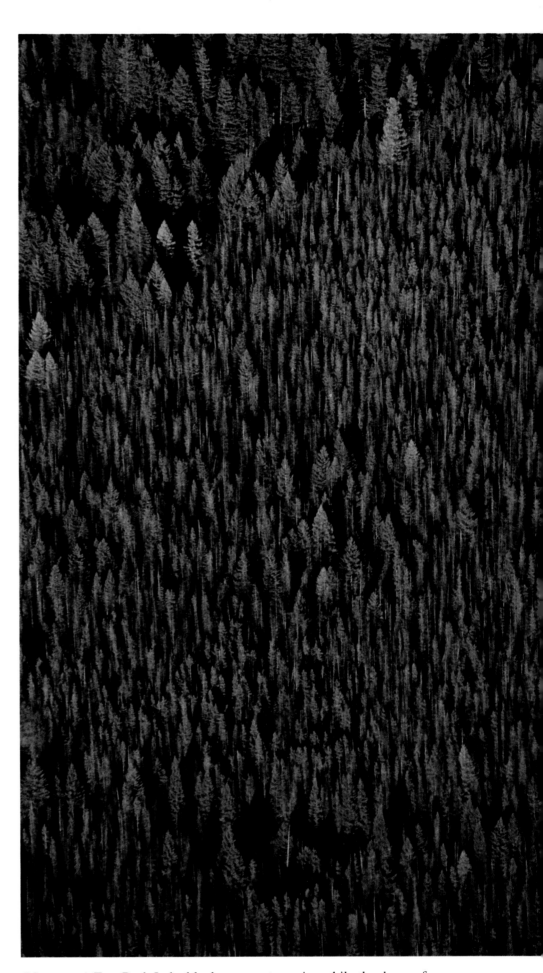

(Above) Light and shadow score earth once hidden by forest. In the succession of evergreen forest in the West, fire is the alpha and the omega. Climax stands of ancient trees bar the sun from reaching the forest floor. Fire, once loosed, rages through the timber, marking the end of one cycle and the beginning of another. Ash fertilizes the soil. Heat bursts rosin-hardened lodgepole pine cones, releasing the seeds of a new generation. Wild flowers and grasses flourish in what was recently the forest's somber depths. Bluebirds, bear and elk congregate in newly created meadows. Meanwhile, seedlings take root and the next generation forest is born.

(Next page) Fort Peck Lake blushes rose at sunrise while the dregs of evening puddle in canyons and nestle along the ridges. This great man-made lake in north-central Montana sprawls behind the largest earth-filled dam in the world.

Cottonwoods stricken by autumn's transformation take their stand along the Missouri River while evergreens retreat into the Breaks.

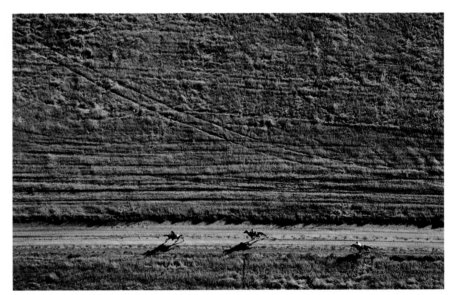

(Top) A sea of gold brushes the edges of the Missouri Breaks near Fort Benton. Fort Benton, which began as a fur trading post and the head of navigation on the Missouri River, survived the death of the steamboats to flourish as the trade center of a great wheat region.

(Above) Crow Indian boys race their horses along a dirt road during Crow Fair. Each year in August, a massive tepee town springs up on the Little Bighorn River near the scene of Custer's Last Stand. The annual pow wow draws Native Americans from across the United States.

A rainbow strikes the earth from a thunderstorm drifting past Springdale. Summer storms, dragging their rumbling bellies across the land, are both a hazard and a spectacle to those who would witness Montana's splendor from the air.

Fog cascading down the Bighorn River near Hardin glistens in the morning sun that will soon burn it away.

Fog flows down cracks and crevices of the Madison River drainage to fill the Bear Trap Canyon Primitive Area west of Bozeman.

Sun and rain are confederates in the mountains where a snow may drench a traveler strolling in bright sunlight. Here sun breaks through a thunderstorm rolling over the Ruby Range near Dillon.

Politicians haggle in Helena, but Downtown Billings is the commercial capital of Montana. Founded by railroad builder Frederick Billings, this south-central Montana city is the distribution center for most of Montana and much of Wyoming.

(Right) The Yellowstone River, struck silver by shards of light from a sunburst in clouds overhead, winds northeast from Custer.

Cradled in the bosom of the Madison Range, glacier-fed Cedar Lake is a relic of the last Ice Age. Lakes like these are often free of ice less than 100 days a year.

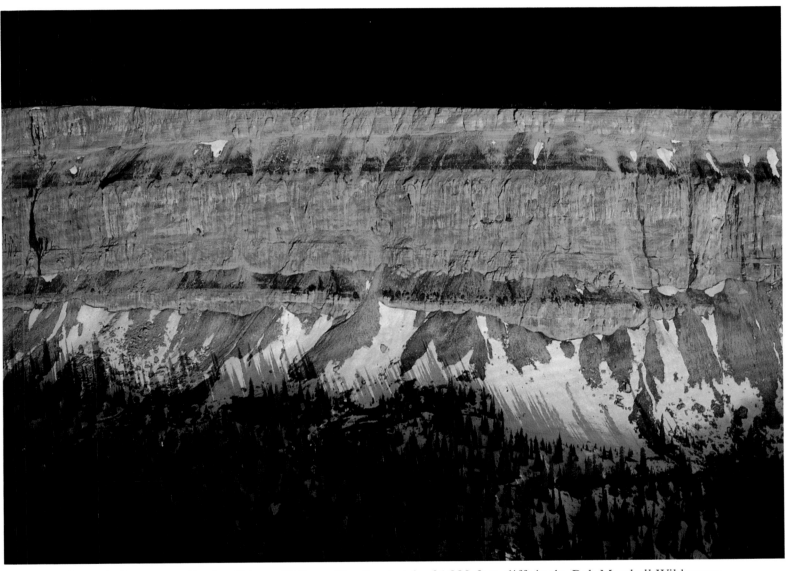

The sun's first rays strike the Chinese Wall, an 18-mile stretch of 1,000-foot cliffs in the Bob Marshall Wilderness. Composed of limestone formed at the bottom of an ancient sea, the wall is one of the most striking stretches of the Continental Divide.

Badland spires carved by wind and rain cluster about Square Butte near the town of Square Butte.

(Above right) Nature's wondrous sandrock sculpture at Medicine Rock State Park near Ekalaka fascinate man today as they did in earlier ages when Plains Indians came here to leave offerings and pray.

(Right) Giant limestone spikes cluster like stone gnomes at the feet of Square Butte. Once the bottom of an ancient sea, this formation was thrust upward millions of years ago.

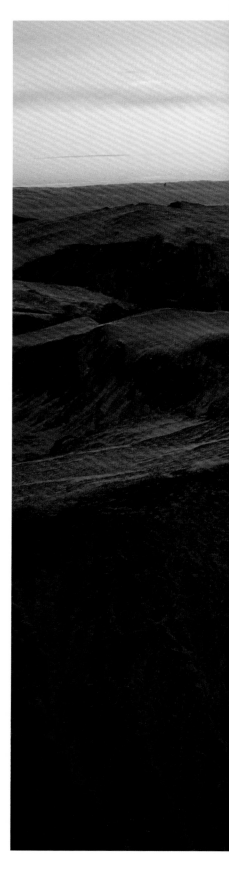

Meandering creeks carve water-lush valleys in the midst of arid hills and scorched prairies in Montana. Ash and willow nestle in the bends of this one near Stanford. Incidentally, Montanans write "creek" but say "crick."

Dawn erupts between crags in the Beartooth Mountains. Location of the state's highest peaks, the Beartooths are home to the grizzly bear and a favorite recreation area for south-central Montanans.

A truck rumbling down a gravel road near Savage pulls a contrail of dust. Junipers fleck the slopes of the breaks beyond while grass cured a golden brown fills the foreground.

Sagebrush burns in a sodbusting operation near Winnett. Plowing virgin prairie sparked pride in early settlers, but more recent sodbusting became the focus of heated controversy as grasslands bypassed as too fragile by the pioneers were plowed by modern corporate farmers.

An assortment of odd birds, the military aircraft on display at Billings Big Sky
International Airshow draws crowds of civilians eager for a close look.

Rodeo is more than a sport in Montana, it's a fiesta, a high point of the summer. More than one bronc
rider will swear he has had seen this view of the Livingston Roundup rodeo arena.

(Next page) Cottonwood and willow groves covering sandbars and islands amid the Yellowstone River
burn gold in the autumn sun near Park City. Captain William Clark and his men marched down the
Yellowstone River from headwaters of the Missouri River in search of trees big enough to make dugout
canoes. At Park City the larger eastern cottonwood begins to replace the slender western cottonwood
of the river's upper reaches.

The ocean of air enveloping Montana can be as rugged as the land below or as smooth as calm water. Here air racers fly their World War II vintage AT6 aircraft over the Gallatin Valley. The land below is magnificent, but the topography of the aerial road is invisible.

(Top left) His face distorted by the rush of wind, skydiver Mark Balsinger prepares to become a part of the Big Sky in a plunge earthward over Bozeman.

(Top right) Cowmen trailing cattle north from Texas were assured their cattle would find ample feed and sweet water if they reached this portion of the upper Yellowstone Valley. Drovers called it "Paradise." Here, hang glider pilot Dan Gravage of Livingston inspects the Paradise Valley from the air.

(Above) Dozens of brightly colored balloons dot a field at Miles City during the annual hot-air balloon roundup. The event draws balloonists from throughout the United States and Canada.

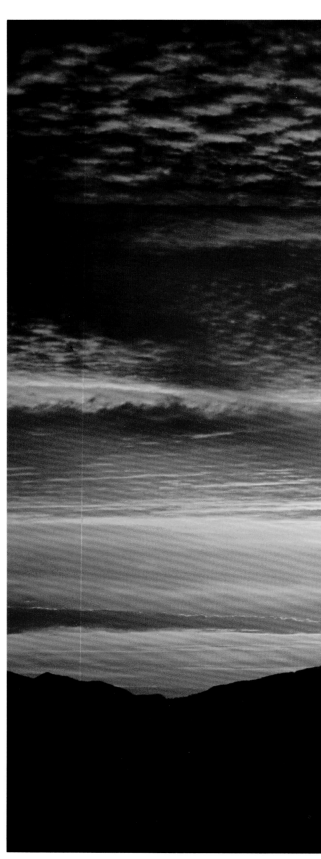

(Above left) A hot air balloon rides unseen currents over the Gallatin Valley near Belgrade. Pastures and cropland of one of Montana's most productive regions sleep beneath winter's snow.

Indians called this lush area "snow hole," living and hunting here in summer but avoiding winter's deep snows. Today residents of Lewistown, a city named for Major William H. Lewis who established a fort there in 1874, enjoy four seasons at the geographic center of the state.

Sun's entry into a new day turns clouds to bronze and silhouettes the mountains of the Bob Marshall Wilderness.

(Next page) Cloud-garnished Hebgen Lake sprawls at the feet of the Madison Range.

Kalispell, a jewel set in the Flathead Valley, shines in the sun with the Swan Range, Flathead Range and Glacier Park in the background. Natives say this valley is where God will vacation if he finds time.

Wild Horse Island rises in rugged splendor from Flathead Lake. Once an exclusive estate, the island is now a state park and domain of a herd of bighorn sheep.

Winter buries a fir forest in the Mission Mountains. Nature has designed coniferous trees, with their short limbs and conical shape, for the heavy snows of the high country.

Snow frosts rugged breaks near Terry. Nature's abstract of pale earth and high relief, these badlands tell tales of a time when the earth was younger. Fossils littering ridges and arroyos speak of a sea that sprawled from the present Rocky Mountains to the Great Lakes region.

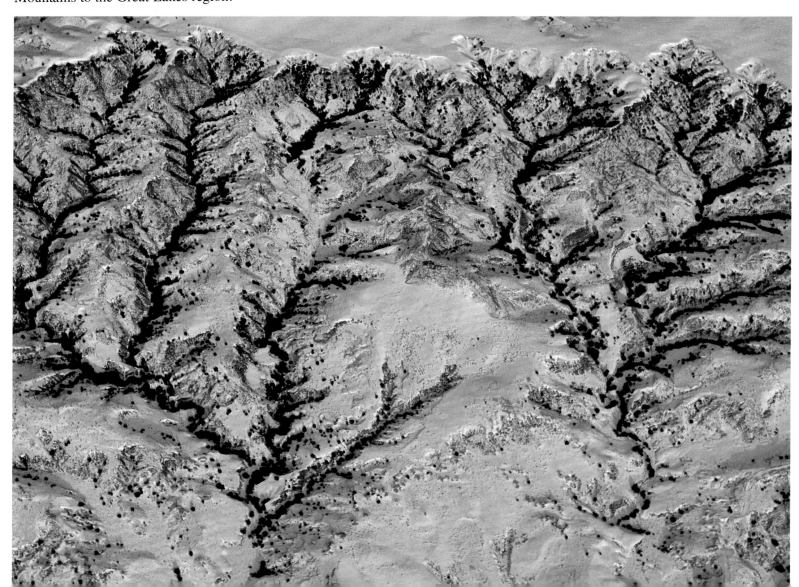

Hay dries in windrows wound in a maze on the floor of the Flathead Valley. In the upper right, a hay baler grazes where Chief Charlo's ponies once grew fat. Home of the Salish and Kootenai, the Flathead Valley was first invaded by French trappers, then by the Jesuits of Father DeSmet.

Great slabs of ice, jumbled by freezing and thawing, thatch Martinsdale Reservoir.

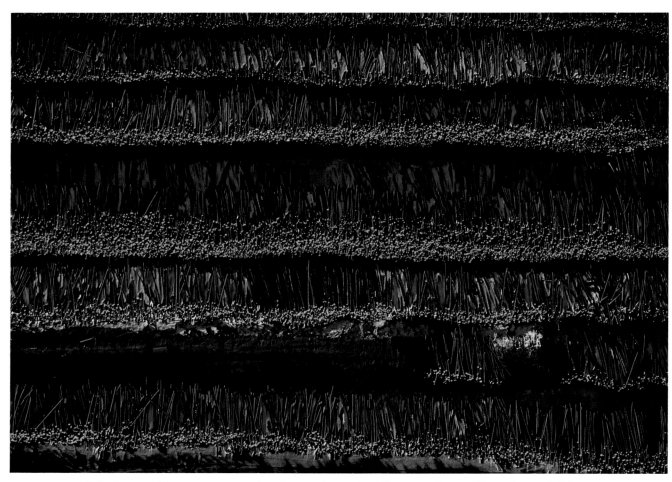

Windrows of logs appear as ripening grain against the snow in a mill yard near Libby.

Undulating stripes of green and grey represent present, past and future in the wheat fields of the Judith Basin. Verdant bands of the current crop alternate with bare strips that raised last year's crop and will be seeded with next year's.

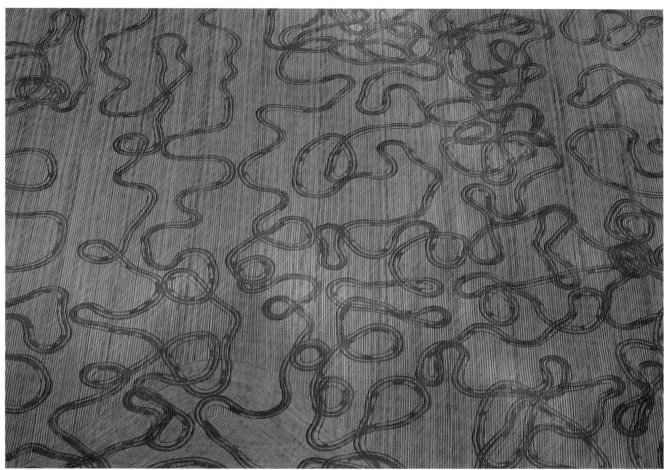

Resembling germs or tapeworms, the maze below is the creation of a farmer plowing near Homestead. Only the farmer knows whether he was inspired, locoed or bored.

Locked beneath a somber lens of ice, Martinsdale Reservoir sleeps through winter while rags of snow cover are torn by the wind. Spring will bring the return of fisherman, the avocet and mallard. Winter is reserved for the gale.

Wedged amid the mountains and cut in half by the Clark's Fork River, Missoula is home of the University of Montana and a major timber industry.

Cowen Peak rises among craggy neighbors in the Absaroka Mountains south of Livingston. Absaroka is a variation of the name Crow Indians call themselves. It means "children of the big beaked bird."

Tracking the winds along the Mission Mountain Range, a single-engine Cessna skims past granite ridges, a cascading stream and a hanging valley. Snow lingers late in these highlands. Glaciers extend their hold in winter and retreat in summer.

A braided Missouri River
skirts islands and mud flats on the
upper reaches of Canyon Ferry Lake
near Townsend.

Massive coal-fired steam plants at Colstrip generate electricity for homes and factories from Montana to San
Francisco. Eastern Montana's coal reserves represent more energy than all the oil beneath Saudi Arabia.

Tepees, arbors and wall tents mark the camps of Crow Indian families at the annual Crow Fair. The fair is an occasion for family reunions, celebration and courting.

Trackless snow smothers a homestead where hope once flourished, then withered and died. Drought and depression extinguished the dreams of thousands of small farmers lured to the West by the promise of free land.

Pelicans shingle the sky over the
Missouri River. Mute, with a wing span of up
to nine feet, the American white pelican
congregates in "bachelor flocks" of
non-breeding young birds on the upper
Missouri.

The Yellowstone River gleams like
burnished silver below the Intake Dam near
Glendive where a fisherman fights rough
waters in pursuit of sauger, bass, catfish or
the giant paddlefish.

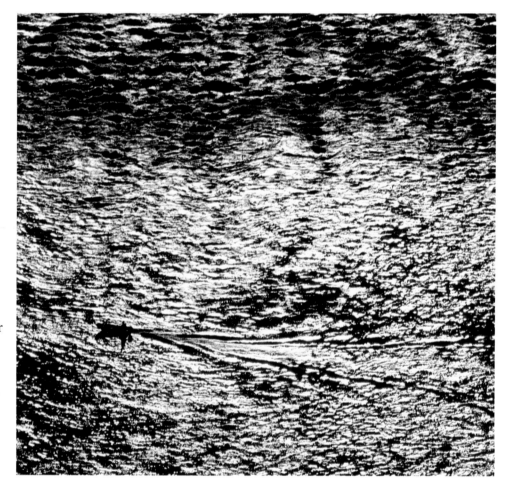

Fishermen seen through a lacework of clouds share Ennis Lake with a lone swan, lower left.

(Below) Paddlefish, living fossils unchanged by millions of years, draw fishermen to Intake Diversion Dam on the Yellowstone River northeast of Glendive. Anglers use deep-sea gear to take fish weighing up to 100 pounds during paddlefish spawning season each year.

(Next page) Chief Mountain, sacred to Indians of this region, breaks the sky near the Canadian border in Glacier Park. Ranchers of southern Alberta joke, "The mountain belongs to Montana, but the view is ours."

Fog swaddles a patch of timber near Ennis Lake.

Like the plains of Eastern Montana, the mountains of Western Montana seem to go on forever. Snow clings to ridges in this sawtooth vista of the Bob Marshall Wilderness.

St. Ignatius basks in the sun against a backdrop of the Mission Mountains. St. Ignatius began as a mission built by Jesuits under Belgian Father Pierre-Jean DeSmet. Named for the founder of their order, the mission remains a religious center for Indians of the Flathead Valley.

A hot-air balloon flaunts its splendor over sugar beet fields. Montana's sugar industry sweetened its cultural heritage. Russian, Germans, Norwegians, Belgians, Mexicans and Japanese came as sugar beet farmers or field workers.

(Right) Combines graze in single file on wheat fields near the old steamboat port of Fort Benton. These lumbering steel behemoths chase the ripening of the grain from Texas up the Great Plains into Montana and on into Saskatchewan and Alberta, Canada.

A tractor follows a green track during sugar beet harvest in the Yellowstone Valley near Sidney. Beet sugar became a strategic substitute for cane sugar during World War II.

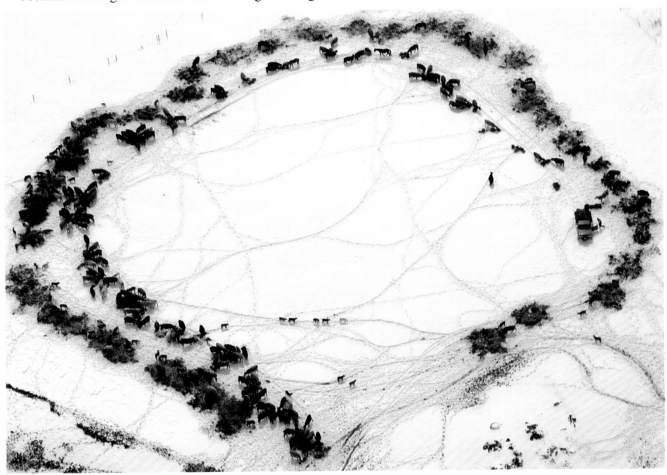

(Left) A farmstead, an island in a sea of grain, stands in the lee of a sheltered belt near the ragged seam where the farmer's world meets the Missouri Breaks near Fort Benton.

(Above) Cattle bawl in gratitude as a rancher scatters hay to feed his livestock after a snowstorm near Lewistown. Early cattlemen, immigrants from the Southwest, allowed their stock to fend for themselves. Massive losses during the winter of 1886-87 ended the days of the open range.

Trailing fog across a massive wheat field, a farmer near Circle sprays a crop raised on a prairie where Crow Indians once warred with the Blackfeet.

Through the brushed gold of an autumn cornfield near Sidney, a farmer chases the grain that will fatten livestock this winter.

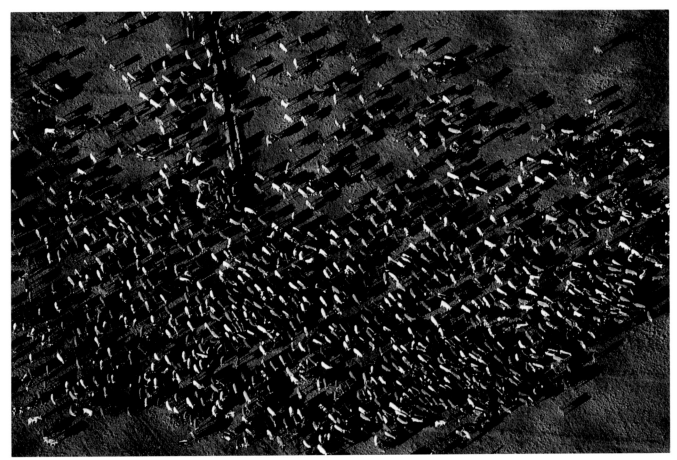

Cattle and cowboys were the major players in the dramatic settlement of Montana's plains. A heritage stretching back to the herds trailed north from the Southwest in the 1860s was celebrated in the Great Montana Centennial Cattle Drive of 1989.

Cars abandoned at the bottom of the mountain await the return of skiers who have fled to the slopes of Bridger Bowl north of Bozeman. Powder snow peculiar to the Rocky Mountains makes Montana skiing some of the finest in the world.

Nature, seemingly at war with herself, carves the magnificent badlands of Makoshika State Park near Glendive. Here the history of eons past is recorded in layers of sea mud and fossils.

Cottonwoods blaze gold in the autumn sun along the Yellowstone River. Nature favors this valley with crisp nights and balmy days in October.

(Right) Light snow cover frosts Pryor Mountain ridges outlined in canyons. Wild mustangs and elk range these arid highlands once occupied by paleolithic hunters. Here, a human history of more than 7,000 years can be read in flint chips and arrowheads.

Great Falls, trade center of Montana's Golden Triangle wheat region, was founded in 1883 at the Great Falls of the Missouri River opposite the mouth of the Sun River.

Anaconda, the smelter city that once processed copper ore from nearby Butte, was once a candidate to be Montana's capital city.

(Above) The Berkeley Pit, a 1,000-foot-deep open pit copper mine, yawns from what was once called "The Richest Hill on Earth" at Butte. The pit was abandoned and is now filling with water after devouring much of the original city.

(Next page) Sawtoothed crags of Glacier National Park once marked the western edge of land ruled by the sister tribes of the Blackfeet, Blood and Piegan.

(Above) A jam on the Yellowstone River shunts muddy water through flood channels past a mosaic of ice floes. Spring breakup and summer floods are the river's most dynamic periods. In these active times the river writhes and leaves its bed to carve new channels, swallow ancient islands and create new ones.

(Right) A motor boat carves watery hieroglyphics on the face of Flathead Lake.

Bozeman, sitting beneath the Bridger Mountains a short distance from navigable portions of both the Yellowstone and Missouri Rivers, became a commercial hub and agricultural center for the gold fields farther west. Today, the city is home of Montana State University and the center of a farm-ranch region.

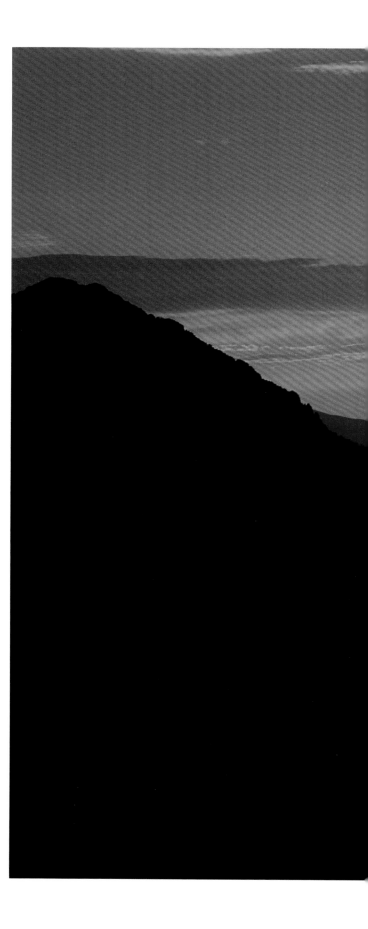

Sunrise explodes over the Bridger Mountains. Night huddles in the lowlands as dawn burns the dew from these heights. At day's end, when darkness has once again settled into the draws and valleys, the sun's last light will be seen on the obverse face of these peaks.

Autumn leaves light the shores of the Milk and Missouri Rivers at their confluence between Glasgow and Wolf Point.

Havre, named for the French seaport Le Havre, was founded by the builders of the Great Northern Railroad. Havre became a bustling railhead and farm center between the Milk River and Bearpaw Mountains where Nez Perce leader Chief Joseph surrendered.

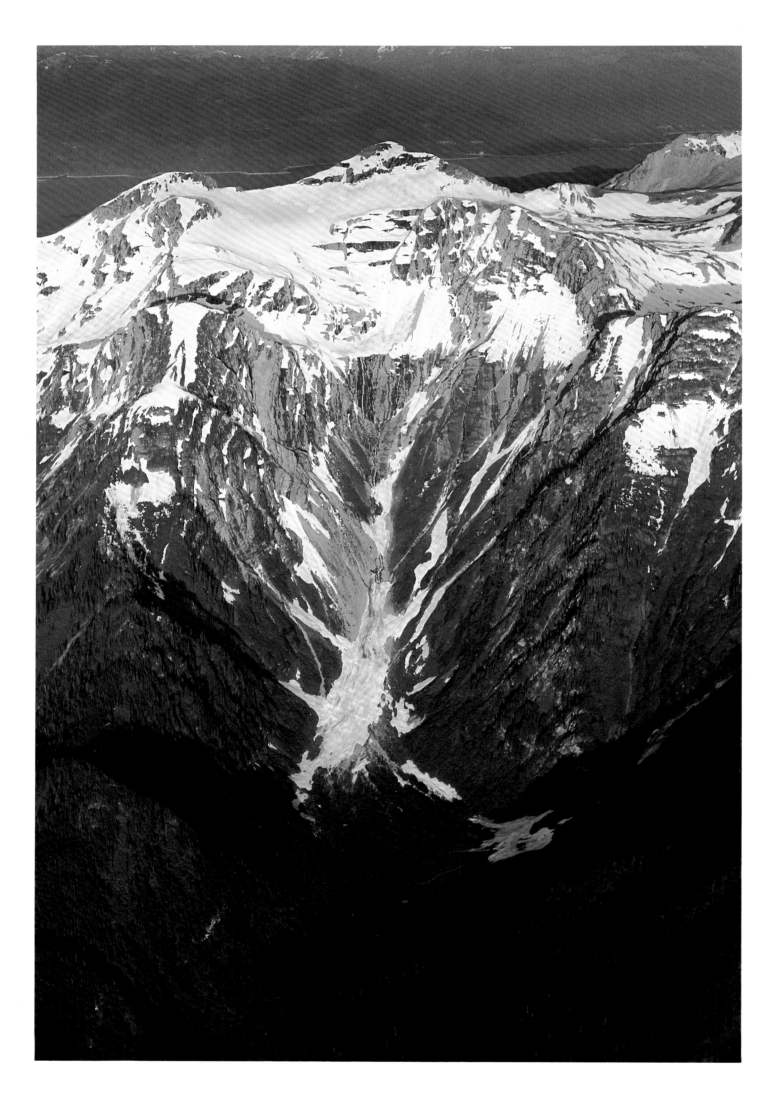

(Above) Sun-shot clouds scatter beams of light and bars of shade over the earth below. These natural pyrotechnics were captured over Rock Creek Valley near Red Lodge.

(Next page) Floodlights illuminate the slopes of Big Mountain Ski Area near Whitefish as night rises from valleys already enveloped in darkness.

(Left) White on ocher, snow clings to the heights of the Flathead Range. Summer runoff from these lofty snow fields feed streams and provide irrigation water for fields and pastures far below.

The reflection of clouds over Glacier National Park's Lake McDonald sandwiches the flying photographer between sky above and sky below.

(Right) Crazy Mountain foothills, like the wrinkled hide of a great green pachyderm fall away from the mountains in creek-laced cattle country.

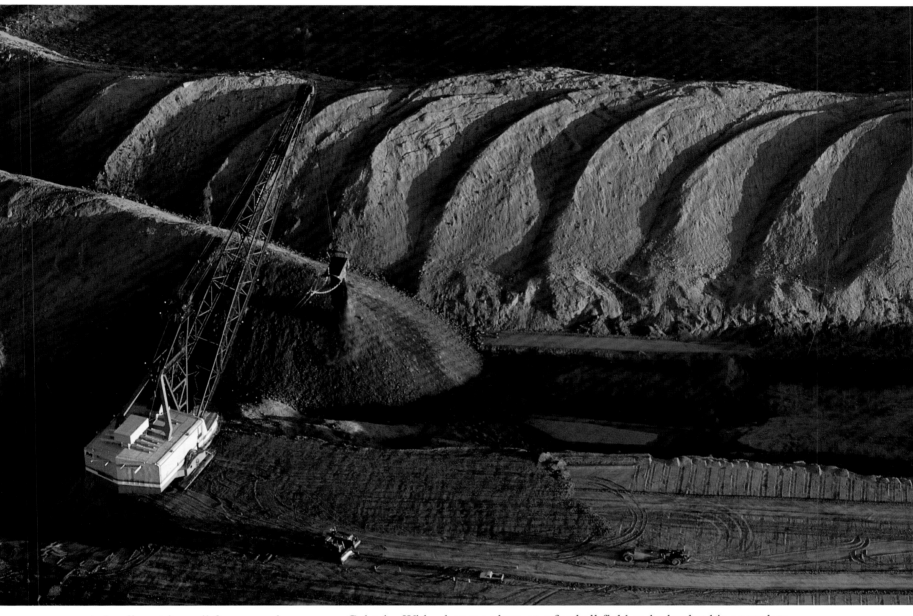

A dragline strips soil from a coal seam near Colstrip. With a boom as long as a football field and a bucket big enough to hold city buses, the mechanical titan dwarfs nearby vehicles.

(Left) Foothills of the Pryor Mountains on the Crow Indian Reservation provide prime cattle pasture, interrupted by clear flowing streams lined with ash, willow, wild rose and chokecherry.

The Flathead River carves a great sweeping bend below Kerr Dam. The river wanders through a valley that was once a great lake created by a glacial dam during the last Ice Age.

Red Rock River scrawls its signature near Red Rock Lakes. Majestic sandhill cranes return each year to feed in meadows wrapped in the bends of this wandering stream. Trumpeter swans, once in danger of extinction, found refuge and thrived on the lakes.

St. Labre Mission on the Tongue River is the spiritual home and alma mater of many Northern Cheyenne Indians. A modern church, built in the shape of a buffalo hide lodge, features an altar with a statue of Christ as a Cheyenne dog soldier.

The Yellowstone River plays wavering counterpoint to the Burlington Northern railroad's straight spine at Glendive.

(Above) Jackson nestles in the Big Hole Valley as clouds from the distant mountains dapple the flats in a camouflage pattern of light and shade.

(Left) Montana's capitol building in Helena gleams beneath a copper dome. Inside, walls of Tennessee marble and massive banisters capture the flavor of 19th Century opulence. The equestrian statue in front of the building portrays Thomas Francis Meagher, Irish revolutionary who came to America to become a Union general in the Civil War. After the war he became acting governor of Montana Territory.

(Next page) A thunderstorm, summer's wonder, rumbles through the foothills. Dragging its sodden footprint through arid grasslands, it plays to an audience of the Absaroka and Beartooth Mountains.

A bench sprawling not far from the Canadian border near Outlook is farmed to the fringe of badlands breaks. Green bars of this year's wheat crop alternate with golden bands of last year's stubble. Color, of course, is an element of Montana's beauty, but so, too, is texture.

Shadows from slowly drifting clouds cast an eerie mosaic pattern over the prairie south of Terry.

Sphinx Peak soars to naked heights above timberline in the Madison Range.

Worshiping in God's country, ranchers and their families congregate close to the Crazy Mountains at the oldest Lutheran Church in Montana near Melville.

(Next page) From high above the Beartooth Mountains, the pilot captures a vista few have seen, the ice and granite world of the Absaroka-Beartooth Wilderness above the timber line.

Lights from Billings gleam as scattered jewels in the Yellowstone Valley as the winter sun buries itself in the Beartooth Mountains.

Haying in the Big Hole Valley is a major summer occupation. The Big Hole is the heart of Western Montana's cattle country.

A tractor pulls its dust plume across the rich Yellowstone River bottomlands near Sidney. Sugar beets, alfalfa, corn and small grains flourish in the loam that eons ago lay beneath a lake formed where the Yellowstone met advancing glaciers.

Old cars, steel steeds that raced Montana's highways and traced her county roads and back country trails, rust in an automobile graveyard. Hidden from those on the ground by high fences, they are seen as a colorful collage from the air.

A spray plane drags a banner of fog across wheat fields south of the Yellowstone Valley near Laurel. Montana hard red winter wheat is prized by millers for its high protein content and excellent milling quality.

A Cut Bank farmer paints the plowed prairie a darker hue. Summer fallowing breaks the surface and kills weeds to preserve moisture. Rain and snow banked this year will help produce next year's wheat crop.

Eagles rule a fantasy world far above the Montana plain. This is the other side of the Big Sky, where mountains grow and dissolve in minutes and monsters rise from milky seas.

The town of Seely Lake sleeps along the shore of the body of water of the same name. Glaciers of the last Ice Age carved this and many other smaller lakes.

Sun on water glows warmly in soft pastels as evening settles on the Medicine Lake National Wildlife Refuge. Birds both rare and common seek refuge here. Tundra swans and whooping cranes pause in their migrations. White pelicans, gulls, and shore birds raise their broods here.

Motorboat wakes stripe the emerald green of Bighorn Lake. Running this course before the mountains rose, the Bighorn River cut through the limestone as the earth thrust it skyward to form the Bighorn and Pryor Mountains.

Mountains, like rows of sharks' teeth, fade into the distance. The Pioneer Mountains loom in the foreground, the Tobacco Root Range fills the background.

Shards of sunlight break through peaks of the Lewis Range, chasing night from the lowlands and turning streams to silver as morning dawns in Glacier National Park.

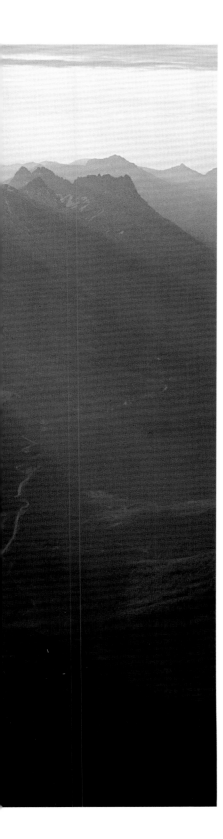

Dusk settles on Miles City, cow capital of Montana. Miles City grew up around Fort Keogh two years after Sioux, Cheyenne and Arapaho overran Lt. Col. George Armstrong Custer and his 7th Cavalry on the Little Bighorn. Texas cowmen trailed longhorns through these streets. The last Cheyenne holdouts surrendered here. Stacks of buffalo hides waiting for steamboats once hid the town from the river. Miles City's past is celebrated each year during the Bucking Horse Sale.

Peaks of the Cabinet Mountains, like whitecaps on a somber sea, tear the Montana sky.

(Right) Stony veins of the Madison Range track through grass and timber of the lowlands to snow-covered heights.

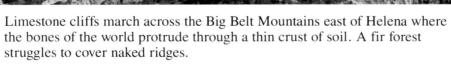
Limestone cliffs march across the Big Belt Mountains east of Helena where the bones of the world protrude through a thin crust of soil. A fir forest struggles to cover naked ridges.

The Missouri River meanders through the Missouri River Breaks. Up this stream came the Lewis and Clark Expedition. Keelboats later carried furs and gold to St. Louis. Steamboats plowing upstream brought settlers and supplies. Until the advent of the railroad the Missouri was Montana's major highway.

(Next page) A tug bulls its way through logs scattered like jackstraws on a mill pond near Libby. The timber industry is to Western Montana what the cattle business is to Eastern Montana.

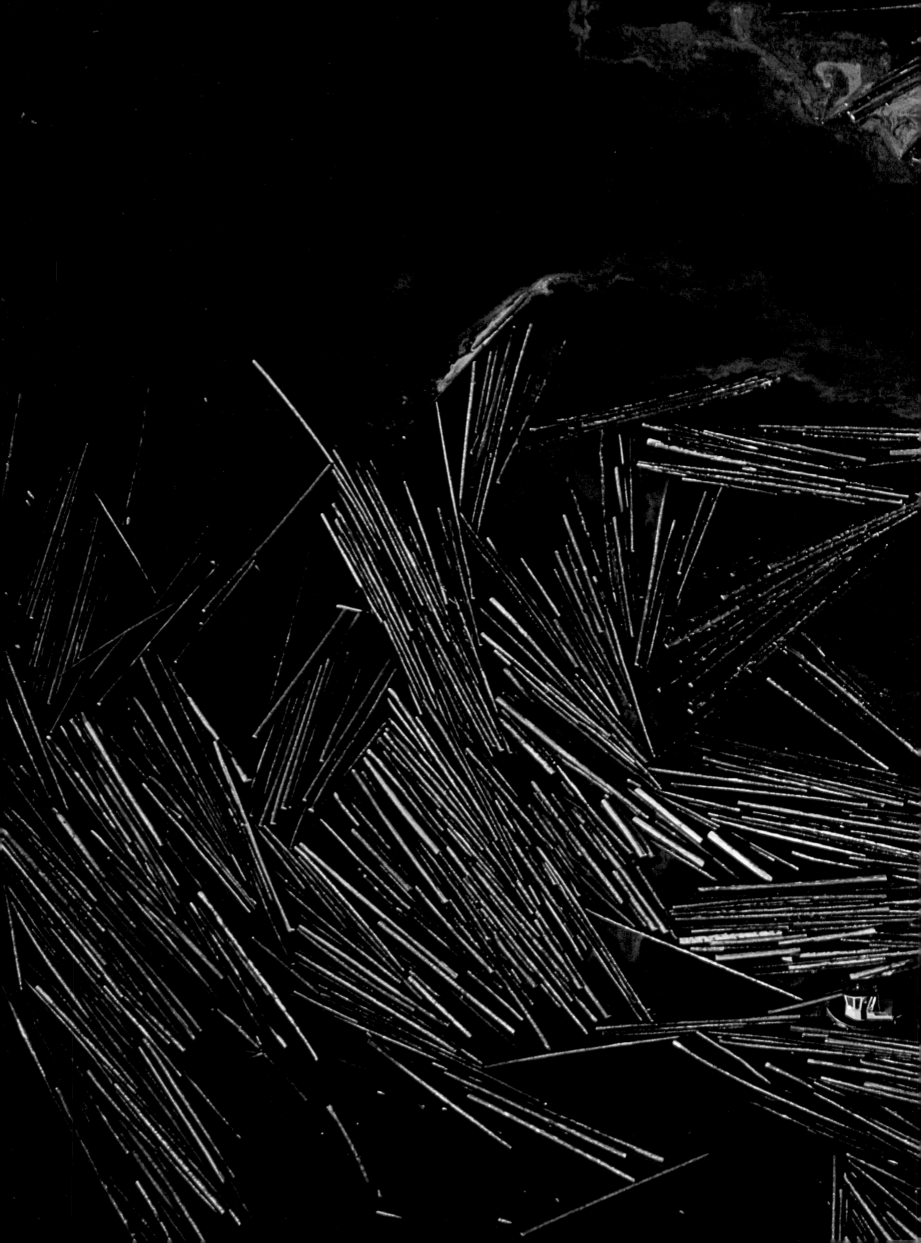

(Below) A sailboat runs close to the wind on Canyon Ferry Lake near Helena. This man-made lake on the Missouri River is a prime recreation area close to the state capital.

Four prospectors from the Confederate South wandered into the Helena Valley in 1864. Exhausted and dispirited, they resolved to try once more for gold. Striking it rich in a draw they named "Last Chance Gulch," they founded the city that would become Montana's capital.

(Left) Bright lights, wild rides, cotton candy, hot dogs and lemonade spell summer fun on the carnival midway at the State Fair in Great Falls.

Ski trails snake through fir groves at Bridger Bowl Ski Trail in the Bridger Mountains near Bozeman.

Limestone cliffs of the Chinese Wall undulate through the Bob Marshall Wilderness. Motor vehicles are banned from the roadless wilderness. Those who come to worship nature at the foot of the wall arrive on foot.

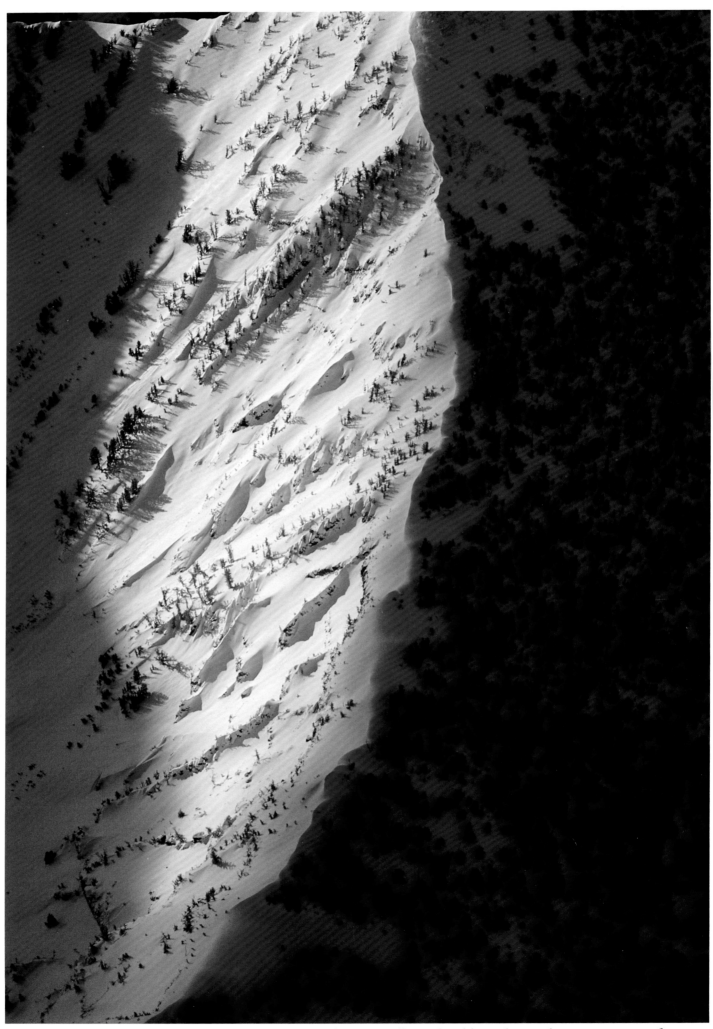

Wind feathers snow along a ridge in the Crazy Mountains. According to local legend, a mad woman ran away from a passing wagon train, thus giving the mountains their name. In summer, wind whistling through gorges and canyons creates a sound of crazed laughter here.

A special passenger train winds its way east of Great Falls during the state's Centennial. Railroads wrote their own chapter of Montana's history, filling the state with settlers and building scores of towns and cities.

A thunderstorm lights the sky over a valley where a trim Interstate 90 races the braided Yellowstone River near Springdale.